BOUNCE
HOUSE

BOUNCE HOUSE

Poems

Jennica Harper

§

WITH ILLUSTRATIONS BY
andrea bennett

ANVIL PRESS :: VANCOUVER

Library and Archives Canada Cataloguing in Publication

Title: Bounce house : poems / by Jennica Harper.
Names: Harper, Jennica, author.
Identifiers: Canadiana 20190088729 | ISBN 9781772141405 (softcover)
Classification: LCC PS8565.A6421 B68 2019 | DDC C811/.6—dc23

Cover design & interior illustrations by andrea bennett
Interior by HeimatHouse
Author photo by Pardeep Singh
Represented in Canada by Publishers Group Canada (Distributed by Raincoast Books); in the U.S. by Small Press Distribution

The publisher gratefully acknowledges the financial assistance of the Canada Council for the Arts, the Canada Book Fund, and the Province of British Columbia through the B.C. Arts Council and the Book Publishing Tax Credit.

Anvil Press Publishers Inc.
P.O. Box 3008, Main Post Office
Vancouver, B.C. V6B 3X5
www.anvilpress.com

PRINTED AND BOUND IN CANADA

for Judy & Dinah

To the dead, anger is like a trampoline, it has bounce.
— "The Dead Ones," MXT, Sina Queyras

Might as well jump. Jump!
—Van Halen

My daughter's resting state is desperate to
bounce. Castles, mini-tramps, the mildest

spring in a playground floor. The new sofas,
of course. D. leaps, unthinking, wants to leave

the Earth one foot at a time, moonwalk steps,
until our umbilical jolts her back to me.

The girl has no interest in following orders.
Much like my mother & her Irish goodbye.

The basketball stars are coming out as flat-
Earthers: they can't see the horizon's curve.

When they jump, they land on their feet &
it's true you can't trust what books tell you.

If you spend every waking hour with a ball, you
need to believe there's more to the world, or less.

At play gym, D. tries to stand on a basketball;
the last fall won't convince her, nor the next.

Crossing the first hospital room's threshold,
we'd donned masks, gown, gloves. Like fathers

about to meet newborns on the other side
of a curtain. Instead, we'd leaned over Mom's

bones in a blanket — wondering if she was
asleep or just stoned. I'd had plans: a new job,

a party, a play. A ticket home, a ticking clock.
We'd sat, prepared to wait, but for how long.

Grief doesn't come as hot or cold like I'd
expected. Not a spike or a pulse, a twist or

·cut. It doesn't cast shade, thrust me under
dark water, prickle my skin. It cycles, repeats

beats: notes not meant to be held. It comes
as quiet: a gentle, total emptiness that eats

meaning, minutes, plans. It is a hole, with
entry & exit unknown. For now, I let it in.

Later many ask if we were close. They mean
post womb, post breast. They mean how long

was the cord, how viscous the blood? My
answer: thick & sticky, yes, but I could

live without. Days, if not weeks. Do I pass?
This is not a test, the world reminds me.

There is no one keeping score, no matter
how often I raise my hand for praise/scorn.

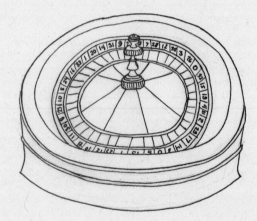

D. is fixated on wounds. The ragged bolt of
white across my palm. M.'s abdominal dots,

a laparoscopic Orion's belt. If she only knew
about the treasures on the average knee. She

likes to touch scarred ridges, doesn't shy away
from the ugly, healing flesh of our rinds: seams

holding our bags of molding straw together. We
planted a sunflower, potted hope. Yet dirt persists.

When Mom was in her third room I'd heard
from a brother & sister she'd cared for

at twenty. Both had photos of "her lake,"
a shoddy birthday cake, a bikini tan &

stories about the boys who'd wanted to date
her. *She was our Maria*, the woman had said.

Except she didn't marry our father, joked
the man. They'd left paperbacks. Questions.

I often think of her lying there, mute, teeth
safe in a locker somewhere. Body on pause,

the weeks X'd off the calendar, a blur. All I
could do was hold her hand, purple & plump

with fluid. Me, sore from my pratfall in the
Halloween aisle of Wal-Mart — bruised ribs,

yes, but more from lying winded on the freshly
waxed floor, as D. looked down on me, unsure.

In '09, we'd played out the reverse: I'd laid
in a bed for thirteen days as they'd tried

to unplug a duct (a stone got stuck). Hair
matted, my fresh-bought engagement ring

home with J. I was not myself — or I was
nothing but myself. She'd called my grim

room every night, we'd talked tests & *House*
& what was next. She'd mommed me to rest.

I've spent months collecting bodily failure
and collapse. Other mothers & lovers seizing,

crushed, metastasizing. I won't lie: they help.
The faithful take solace in their loved one's

uniqueness, but I want my loss anonymous.
She could have been anyone, there was no hand

reaching down & plucking her from her bed. Only
a wheel that spins black or red, black or red.

Why didn't she wait? I'd said I was coming.
I'd gone anyway. Took the Friday red eye,

slept just fine without wine. Then West on
the 401where I'd followed the dotted line

to her apartment, the emptiest of nests.
Quiet except for the budgie overhead,

squawking to be fed. She couldn't wait
— but then, I'd said she didn't have to.

Why am I so sure the Earth is round? I've
never seen it, tiny, from my shuttle window.

To the flat-Earthers, a globe is only as real
as a pile of tortoises; each ridge a mountain.

Nevertheless, there's an appeal to flatness.
It might be a relief to walk a map, to know

forward from back, wood from desert. How
long the journey will be & that it will end.

Two days after she died, B. & I had ran-
sacked Mom's pad. I'd found her pearls,

Grandma's pearls, really, creamy & small
in a green clamshell box shaped like

a smile or a woman's throat. B. had taken
a shine to a cache of world currency,

coins she never spent. But she'd worn
the pearls. You can take that to the bank.

Between my brother & me, babies. There
had been two but two'd become none.

We name J. because he'd breathed, because
she'd named him, because he was one of us.

The cat in the box is neither dead nor alive —
there is no cat. Only men & their theories.

D. plays with nesting dolls, puts the middle
child in upside-down, gets him stuck.

Most of my life I mistook her for shy.
In fact, she was the belle of most balls,

her shiny curls (twisted in cloths overnight)
stayed tight as she danced, no mean feat.

I would like to swivel back — fifty years
might be enough. To see her on her feet,

spheres of honeyed light dappling the floor,
as she's wooed by a boy she's too good for.

She'd had to sort the poker chips. Stack
them by colour, tidy silos on the Ace-King

& the 7-8-9, where they'd piled high
waiting to be almost-but-not-quite won.

She'd needed no poker face, never raised
just to fluff the pot. Everyone knew not

to trash talk her. There was no point. She
only bet when she'd had a house or higher.

Her life in boxes. A garage of pages: the letter
from the bank explaining the garnishee of her

wages. Decades' worth of birthday cards,
Mother's Day, our store-bought, brief hellos.

Along with first drafts of each letter she'd ever
sent: years of love, pleas, then rage at his debt

& at not being a parent. Finally, her flourish:
she'd have another one, with or without him.

Two churches in one day: a ceremony, then
the reception. Her college neighbourhood &

mine. Long lines at the liquor store, for sushi,
for the walk-in (since every day is someone's

morning after). The cousins here are kind but
I don't recognize any of their faces. For the first

time, my feet are the ones dancing as tiny
shoes cling on. We shuffle, spin. Hold the line.

Down a well-used gravel road, past the rest
home Mom had briefly toured & quickly hated,

D. & I visit the butterfly conservatory: faux-
Amazon off the dusty highway. I see creepy

crawlies, just prettier. D. loathes them flying
near her, but when we get to the end there's

a bowl of mismatched broken wings, & she sticks
her hand right in: riffles through soft specimens.

D. could get hit by a car while I push her
stroller across the street. Or teeter off

the couch, crack her skull. She could catch
a shoelace in escalator slats, slip from the sea

wall into black water. Or get attacked by
geese: vile motherfuckers. She plays "kite"

with the blind cords, eyes triple-A batteries.
Plus sometimes I feed her expired mayonnaise.

A long ago road, en route to a Spring Break
beach, we're betrayed by old All-Seasons & a

slick sudden snow. First the slide across four
lanes, then a roll. In the ditch, we hang by our

belts — astronauts but the float hurts —
almost as much as the unbuckle & fall.

My mother, the driver, more bruised than us
saying she's sorry, so sorry, it's all her fault.

As she'd gotten older she'd paid for perms
to plump up her 'do, hide the ears she'd

always thought stuck out — though none
of us had seen it. An offhand critique from

her mother that lives on. D.'s hair won't grow
beyond her ears, just hits her nape, doubles

back on itself into unkempt fluffy curls. Mom
would have killed for those curls, or died.

Now, another mother in another bloody
room. The bleached air & fear, the bad

food. I wonder, have I had too much for too
long? Is it time to step aside, let someone else

have joy, comfort, an obligatory call to make
twice a week? Show me the log book, we'll

divide & conquer. Someone out there needs
a mother, we're going to set this straight.

Winter: I want to say she'd loved skaters'
spins most — blades carving ohs in ice

until only fine grooves remained, as if
perfect impressions were the point.

Actually she'd been a sucker for a flip,
or three or four. Less art more sport,

blades chunking, ice flying: the only
divine curve the Russian's muscular ass.

I'd worn her pearls to the funeral.
Dressed in floral, like a woman or

a woman in costume as a woman.
What I thought she'd have liked: bold

print, to the knee, low heels, nude
hose. A far cry from normal, jeans

cuffed, black boots. Laissez-hair.
Holes in lobes long since grown over.

D. has learned the teapot song. I try
not to cringe at *short & stout* — my life

& maybe hers too. No comments please
about toddler thighs, honey-pot tummies,

the fucking Buddha. I don't want you ringing
in her ears, flushing her pinchable cheeks.

I've run the circuit on this, gone round
& round. Spill it. Smash it. Pour it out.

Summer, it was baseball on the radio.
The radio! A tribute to the truly slow

burn. She'd listen on the deck, in
the car, just sit & imagine fly balls

hanging in the air like stars. Her wait
the wait of those watching, the same

soundless pause before a man says it was
caught because they nearly always are.

D. is always looking up — but only
to count the number of bulbs burnt out.

Her indictment of adults. Subscriber
to the broken window theory. A pedant,

really. She doesn't yet know how hard
it is to keep trains running, to stay fed

& rested, to make time to light the world.
The world is always looking for a fight.

The week after D.'s birth she thinned
rapidly, visibly. Milk a trickle, our latch

a bitch. The midwives assured us not
to worry, but her rolls smoothed out

completely, revealed outlines of ribs.
A hole emptied itself in me: *if she loses,*

I will too. Over time she softened. But
I've stayed hard, rage at the ready.

D.'s favourite trust game: she jumps
from the highest stair into my arms

four steps below. Sometimes it's a tip,
sometimes a slow leap — but she never

hesitates. The game is mine, the trust
mine: do I trust myself? To match her

line, to wait where she aims. To catch
the kid landing, not the one at the top.

A childhood stacked with quarters: wax-
wrapped & tucked in birthday cakes,

squirrelled away in homemade ceramic
ducks, pressed in commemorative velvet

(fake, natch) to celebrate vets & jocks.
I'd taken the silver offerings & swallowed

at least two. At the pool, Dad held me by
the ankles, shook till I was no longer blue.

D. joins her cousins on their backyard
trampoline & finds God at three. Suddenly

happy to skip meals indefinitely. Speechless
with the thrill of bounce without end.

At home she has no trampoline, no yard. Just
short flights of stairs, an endless vertical

climb. She'll spend three days here, falling
without consequence, until the rain sets in.

D.'s newest baby doll is smaller
than she'd been when she was born.

Smaller than most preemies even: soft
body, but oddly hard head, hands & feet.

Each night D. tucks her carefully into our
bed (never her own). We forget every time,

find the thing at midnight. I clutch her hard,
this unbreakable baby of plastic & foam.

Mom had been the baby, the litter's runt
(her word, it creeps me out). She'd started

scrawny. But I was baby-round & stayed
that way. Cheeks that begged for a squeeze.

Later it was breasts. A body at rest remains
soft, easy. Right? Don't mistake a girl's soft-

ness for weak-ness. Small is fast & we relish
bursting your bubbles with our tiny fists.

I don't want another child — a second
D. — but wouldn't mind another round

of pregnancy. The mother of excuses,
a card that trumps in any game: Sorry,

I'm painting a room, doing yoga, I'm
feeling her kick, I'm rubbing in creams.

I'm writing down the dreams I have
for her, then *flick*! letting them burn.

The mole that grows.   An edge
that bleeds.   Lesions that bloom,

splotchy masses   on the screen.
Moon-shadows looming;   a bowl

cracked & mended,   upended.
A manhole unlidded. Hell.   A cell

that blossoms: lilies   taking over
this field   & the one beyond.

Cancers in the air. Behind a temple, coursing
through blood, both breasts, again. Yet our

mothers — cell division normal — find other
ways to go. A heart done carrying the dead

weight of a paralyzed half. A slip & hours on
the floor, no one hearing the call. The dice

aren't loaded before you come through the door.
The dice feel nothing but the felt below.

This is not a story. I want to narrativize
but the planks don't meet clean. It's all

slivers & gaps between slats. D. wants
to crawl through the smallest of spaces —

memories of a cephalopod, a poem. I go
back & forth: fear / no fear / fear / no fear

but nothing sticks. Shanks of hair on the floor,
well of contaminated water, mirror of tricks.

Yes, if I'm honest, there is some
relief. No more guilt at visiting only

twice a year, Skyping on birthdays.
No more getting pissy with her for

going too slow, or not knowing what
she needed & just asking for it.

No going to the home that's not
home. Yes. If you're asking. Some.

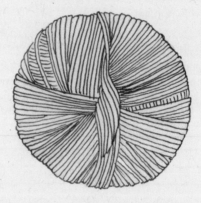

D. has spotted two tiny new marks:
a freckle on her right hip, plus one

on the pad of her left foot. She delights
in her body's surprises ... but I want to

stop the spots, put everything back how
it was, factory settings. I imagine Mom

watching my moles come in, staining my
arms & neck, marring what she'd made.

I don't think I have a recording of her
voice. A thousand of D.'s, none of hers.

How did I let this happen? I'll forget it, I
know I will. Soon have only an idea of it,

the shape of her mouth as it said my name
but not the sound of the word, which is the

word. What's left: letters, a shared allergy,
a handful of objects sculpted of wood.

B. has her organ, rust red & scratched,
& mostly ignored in favour of a newer

model: an electronic piano, within reach
of small hands. But every few days some

boy or man stops to finger the organ's
worn keys. Pulls its stops. Coaxes from its

holes a deep, warm bellow. The days since she
left fill up faster with sand, hours & hours of it.

I gave up the name she first gave me. *Jennifer*.
It was her idea: she wished she'd been braver,

had thought outside the box, had guessed how
many of us there'd be. It's not until D. that I

can imagine the gut-punch of a child rejecting
the first thing you give them. I ask D. which

is her favourite flower? She cups her hand, aims
it down. The ones that turn away from the sun.

Our tiny herb garden is growing, but only,
it seems, the useless shoots. Little dashes,

the ornamentals. Nothing dominant you'd
build a meal around, nothing you can sink

your teeth into. In the deep Arctic, the seed
vault has flooded. No match for melting

permafrost. What was intended to survive,
go on without us, now needs supervision.

This won't ever be done. There's zero
chance of wrapping it up like the boxes

tagged & taped & under the floorboards.
Of divorcing it like a spouse whose heart's

not in it anymore. Here's yet another story
packed with gore & abortion, dogs put down

early, rings down drains. Of lays not easy
to acquire & rarely worth waiting for.

They mock poets for our fixation on
birds. We see ourselves too clearly in

their prehistoric faces. We're small &
bony, aspire too eagerly to flight. Really

they should mock us for our love of trees:
how we flock to their leafy boughs, their

gnarls & hollows, perceived gravitas, how
we get caught in their glorious taxonomy.

Once, within twenty-four hours, I'd washed
both their hair. Each fine & lightly waved,

the saturation darkening, straightening. One
had been a wash of mercy: fingers massaging

a scalp untouched for weeks. Then the other,
to get the guck out, honey & brambles, detritus

of a day not worth remembering — that one had
been a mercy for the washer; for these hands.

D. asks me what her wrinkly belly button
is, what it's for. I tell her the truth: nothing,

anymore. I try to explain, when she was
inside we were connected by a cord & that

cord is how we'd shared food. She tells me
I'm silly. Says she is my Mummy now, she's

going to feed me. I smile & poke her belly.
Press the button. All that's left, this hole.

She'd been alone. After all the visits she'd
woken up one Friday & slipped away.

Is it worse to be alone? I have no way
of preventing it — not marriage, not child

— they may be far away when I slip-slide
into the dark. But maybe it's all right, this

seeing-one's-self-out business. So polite.
Requiring no negotiation, talk of the light.

I've said she couldn't stay, left abruptly,
but where do I think she's gone? I know

where the pieces are. Boxed ash in Douglas
Fir. I have her words, longhand, foolscapped,

accordion-filed. Chronology by pile; a catalogue
of sentiment & rages. Is that her? I glance at D. —

slow but not scared, waiting quiet at the edges
of each moment, circling — & see her there.

The Earth must be round for no other
reason than the fact we invented the wheel.

D. on the back as I pedal my bike, never
more conscious of the hard ground. My

mother in her wheelchair, one foot dragging
her self forward. Both ox & cart. The need

to turn is in our bones: we loop before we
leap. Hope to face forward, come around.

Thank You:

To Michael V. Smith, who edited the manuscript with fierce love.

To Marita Dachsel, for her care and support — of this book, and of me.

To andrea bennett, for her wonderful drawings and cover.

To Brian Kaufman and Karen Green at Anvil Press, for their ongoing friendship and faith.

To my mom, Judith Lynn Harper, who passed away in 2017. And to her close friend Lorna Montgomery, who helped so much through Mom's illness and then became ill herself the following year. You are both so missed.

To my family, especially my brother Ben — who I'm sure would write a different book, but would never ask me not to write mine.

To Jeff and Dinah, for being home.

ABOUT THE AUTHOR:

Jennica Harper is the author of three previous books of poetry: *Wood* (Anvil Press, 2013), which was shortlisted for the Dorothy Livesay prize, *What It Feels Like for a Girl* (Anvil Press, 2008), and *The Octopus and Other Poems* (Signature Editions, 2006). Her poetry has been translated for the stage (*Initiation Trilogy*), gone viral, and won Silver at the National Magazine Awards. Jennica also writes for television, and lives with her family in Vancouver.